A CASE STUDY IN COMMUNITY ORGANIZING

RELENTLESS

Sustaining a Successful People's Campaign to Reform an Entrenched Public Housing Bureaucracy

MICHAEL STANLEY

FOREWORD BY MICHAEL GECAN

RELENTLESS
*Sustaining a Successful People's Campaign
to Reform an Entrenched Public Housing Bureaucracy*

Michael Stanley
Foreword by Michael Gecan

Editing by Gregory F. Augustine Pierce
Cover and text design and typesetting by Andrea Reider

Text copyright © 2024 by Michael Stanley
Foreword copyright © 2024 by Michael Gecan

Published by ACTA Publications, 7135 W. Keeney Street
Niles, IL 60714, (800) 397-2282, www.actapublications.com

All rights reserved. No part of this publication may be reproduced or transmitted in any form or by any means, electronic or mechanical, including photocopying and recording, or by any information storage and retrieval system, including the Internet, without permission from the publisher. Permission is hereby given to use short excerpts with proper citation in reviews and marketing copy, church bulletins and handouts, and scholarly papers.

ISBN: 978-0-87946-738-8
Printed in the United States of America by Total Printing Systems
Year 30 29 28 27 26 25 24 24
Printing 10 9 8 7 6 5 4 3 2 First
Text printed on 30% post-consumer recycled paper

FOREWORD

RELENTLESS INDEED

by Michael Gecan

I remember vividly the first meeting that East Brooklyn Congregations (EBC) had with the then-chair of the New York City Housing Authority (NYCHA), Emmanuel Popilizio, and his top assistant, Joan Wallick, late in 1986. Popilizio was an old-school Democratic operative from Little Italy—savvy, funny, and immovable. Wallick was a new-generation professional administrator who lived in a lovely brownstone in Brooklyn Heights. They were the original odd couple.

Why and how then-Mayor Edward Koch sentenced the two of them to run NYCHA are questions whose answers I never learned. But there they were. And there we were—a relatively new Industrial Areas Foundation (IAF) affiliate trying to draw attention to the challenges that NYCHA tenants faced in Brownsville and East New York.

NYCHA is still a city within a city—177,000 apartments housing approximately 500,000 New Yorkers as of 2024. Its population is greater than the cities of Atlanta, Miami, and Sacramento, according to NYCHA's own website, and about the same as Baltimore and San Francisco. In Brooklyn, approximately 130,000 people call NYCHA home, with similar numbers in Manhattan and the Bronx. The sheer massive scale of the agency is enough to scare the faint of heart away.

But scale isn't the only issue. NYCHA belongs, in essence, to no one: not the city, not the state, not the federal government. Each level of bureaucracy has some role to play in NYCHA, but none exercises clear and accountable control over the actual conditions in the buildings. It's an orphan agency that, historically, was often used as a patronage dumping ground for New York mayors and other elected officials and a honey-pot for all kinds of vendors and service agencies.

These and other realities became clear to me and my two colleagues then on the EBC staff, Stephen Roberson and Lucille Clark, as we began to meet leaders who lived in NYCHA developments, often climbing eight or ten floors because the elevators were broken, navigating gangs who used the lobbies and stairwells as meeting places, avoiding the trash that NYCHA staff had failed to collect. Several of the founding leaders of EBC—Domingo Lind, Sarah Plowden, and others—lived in NYCHA buildings. So we met those leaders, held house meetings in their apartments, identified issues (which IAF has always defined as something that is "immediate, specific, and winnable), and took those issues to Popilizio and Wallick.

To our surprise, they responded, although they were also somewhat bemused. They had seen scores of groups come and go, worn out by the endless list of needs that seemed to surface daily and the often-grudging response of NYCHA staff. Many months later, Wallick, who belonged to an Episcopal church in downtown Brooklyn that later became a member of EBC, met with me and said, "We are trying to respond. But what happens when you leave?" She meant that in a personal way. What might happen when Stephen and Lucille and I disappear—as we surely would, given the history of NYCHA. But she also meant it in an institutional way. What would happen when EBC and IAF disappeared, because every other organization and effort to tackle the NYCHA in a meaningful way had evaporated eventually.

Thirty-seven years later, no one can answer that question. While Stephen, Lucille, and I all moved on, other organizers and, more importantly, the leaders in EBC, Queens Power, South Bronx Churches, and Manhattan Together—all Metro IAF affiliates in NYC, took the baton and kept running the race. Their story in this case study is the very definition of an organizational ultra-marathon.

Over the years, leaders like the Reverend Getulio Cruz, Joanne Kennedy, Ray Lopez, Bernard Smith, and so many others have maintained a steady and relentless series of approaches to addressing the needs of NYCHA tenants. And organizers like Marielys Divanne, Ken Thorbourne, Anna London, Grant Lindsay, Rob English, Robbie Block, and Michael Stanley have trained, supported, and agitated those leaders all along the way.

In IAF, we talk about all organizing as a process of dis-organizing and re-organizing. This account, prepared by Michael Stanley, who emerged as the most experienced and knowledgeable IAF organizer on the NYCHA case, describes that process in detail. *Relentless* is a complicated tale, extending over four decades and involving different angles and approaches that are designed, tested, implemented, and sometimes discarded when a community must win for its own survival against a massive and inert bureaucracy in a place that has given up on the notion that something is so bad that it can never be improved or held accountable by the people it serves.

This case study shows what creative organizing, done with clarity and flexibility, can accomplish. And it proves that the leverage generated by deep, leader-led, citizens power organizations can generate fundamental change in the most difficult of conditions.

But enough background from me. Read this book and learn, read it and weep or laugh or both, and read it and get organized where you are against whomever or whatever is standing in your way.

RELENTLESS

Mike Gecan is the former co-executive director of the Industrial Areas Foundation (IAF) and the co-founder of Metro IAF, which operates east of the Mississippi River. He is the author of *Going Public: An Organizer's Guide to Citizens' Action; People's Institutions in Decline: Causes, Consequences, Cures;* and *Effective Organizing for Congregational Renewal.*

INTRODUCTION

Taking on a Behemoth

One of the greatest challenges that Metro Industrial Areas Foundation power organizations have faced is how to sustain an extended effort—across years and even decades—against large, entrenched bureaucracies. That is the challenge that Metro IAF affiliates in New York City have dealt with over the last four decades in taking on the dysfunction at New York City Housing Authority (NYCHA).

NYCHA includes over 177,000 apartments in 335 developments in all five boroughs. It is home to over 500,000 poor and working poor New Yorkers—a kind of city within the larger city of eight million plus. It also is the nation's largest public housing system and now represents 18% of all public housing in the United States.

As federal support has withdrawn and as administration after administration at the city and state level has failed to address both the immediate and longer-term needs of the system, NYCHA has become a synonym for "crisis," "dysfunction," "mismanagement," and "corruption."

In February of 2024, seventy NYCHA staff members were arrested for taking payoffs in exchange for contracts to various vendors. That is just the latest in a long line of episodes that New Yorkers have read or heard about on a regular basis. In the vacuum left by inadequate management and neglect from mayors and governors, those who see the potential for a windfall have pushed for the privatization of NYCHA developments, while others have suggested billion-dollar schemes that have no grounding in reality.

Meanwhile, the leaders and organizers of Metro IAF affiliates have applied the basic tools of organizing—thousands of individual meetings with NYCHA residents, hundreds of house meetings in apartments and religious and community organizations near NYCHA developments, identifying new leaders and issues of concern, and then organizing disciplined, public actions to get responses.

To augment the on-the-ground organizing, twelve years ago Metro IAF leaders decided to initiate a parallel legal strategy to force the city to respond to one persistent and systemic problem: mold in NYCHA apartments that triggered asthma and other respiratory problems among the very young, the very old, and many tenants in between. This two-pronged approach, led by determined NYCHA tenants, supported by other Metro IAF leaders and organizers, has resulted in documented improvements in 30,000 apartments, as well as an upgrading of security, maintenance, and other areas of concern that for too long had gone unaddressed.

This case study does not tell a heart-warming story of complete, or even nearly complete, victory. While tangible gains have been made, still today too many NYCHA tenants are suffering. What we hope to convey is how four IAF affiliates—with a total organizing staff of nine, but with hundreds of trained and effective volunteer leaders—have been able to create constructive change in a system that so many have either given up on or seen as a punchline at a dinner party.

The focus of this book, instead, will be on the steps that were taken, the decisions made, and the reflections that have occurred over nearly forty years of organizing to improve the quality of life in NYCHA. This paper also seeks to highlight the roles played by a number of important allies, including lawyers from the Natural Resources Defense Council and other public service groups and private firms, data and mold analysts, a senior United States senator, a key United States representative, a federal court, and several journalists who, with Metro IAF, have never thrown in the towel.

Michael Stanley
Metro Industrial Areas Foundation
New York City, New York
Independence Day
July 4, 2024

BACKGROUND AND EARLY YEARS

Organizers working with Metro IAF affiliate East Brooklyn Congregations (EBC) began meeting tenants in various NYC Housing Authority (NYCHA) developments in 1981 and attended the first organizing meeting of NYCHA residents in 1983. A few years later, Queens Citizens Organization (also a Metro IAF affiliate) leaders began to emerge in NYCHA developments in Far Rockaway. The number of leaders and developments in which Metro Industrial Areas Foundation (IAF) had a presence expanded rapidly as Metro IAF affiliates South Bronx Churches and Manhattan Together were founded.

Leaders identified and addressed a range of issues—fixing broken locks on lobby doors; pressing the police department to pay more attention to NYCHA stairwells and open spaces that often became settings for dangerous drug dealing; demanding that maintenance staff respond more promptly to complaints that historically had been ignored. In many developments, leaders grew concerned about the use of a dangerous pesticide in the hallways and lobbies. Press attention to these and other issues led to grudging compliance from NYCHA management. In addition, Metro IAF tenant teams demanded and eventually secured the establishment of centralized tracking of complaints and the start of the systematic scheduling of maintenance appointments, ending decades of frustration since NYCHA tenants never knew if, or when, repair staff would appear. Thousands of immediate issues were resolved in this way.

There were moments of real drama. For example, when Metro IAF invited a top HUD official to tour buildings and view first-hand the conditions residents were facing, the official was trapped— along with several Metro IAF leaders and NYCHA representatives—in a single elevator that broke down. Faulty elevator service was one of the many chronic issues that NYCHA tenants hoped to speak with HUD about, so the timing of that breakdown couldn't have been better.

That particular elevator was fixed in record time, but the problems persisted in scores of NYCHA buildings all across the city.

THE LAWSUIT

A pattern emerged over the years. Metro IAF leaders realized that NYCHA could be forced to respond to any issues spotted and championed by residents in scores of developments. But Metro IAF had a presence in only about 20% of the NYCHA complexes. And that meant that the same issues resolved in a building with Metro IAF tenant teams would go unresolved in the other 80% of NYCHA developments.

In other words, NYCHA proved reactive but never proactive in applying the lessons learned in resolving issues outside of where Metro IAF could demand attention. Further, even in apartments where Metro IAF identified mold infestation caused by leaks and a lack of ventilation, NYCHA might respond by scraping away and then painting over the mold. (This often did not correct the root cause of the problems). But NYCHA would not address the same conditions in dozens of other apartment buildings where tenants either didn't report the problem or simply gave up after years of complaints and no responses. The Metro IAF team knew something else was needed to increase the pressure on NYCHA and create the overall accountability that would force the Authority out of its grudgingly reactive mode.

That something was a lawsuit. In 2011, Metro IAF organizers and leaders approached lawyers Nancy Marks and Al Huang of the Natural Resources Defense Council (NRDC). NRDC had worked effectively to assist a sister Metro IAF organization, the Interfaith Community Organization in Jersey City, in its attempts to force PPG Industries to clean up its toxic waste at the 100-acre Canal Crossings site. The $600 million court-ordered cleanup should be completed in mid-2025. A different $400 million settlement won against the Honeywell corporation at another 100-acre site in the Bayfront site in Jersey City, won with a different legal team, has been completed and the first phase of a proposed 8,000 new housing units (35% of which will be affordable housing) is now under construction. When Canal Crossings is remediated, it too will then be able to support thousands of desperately needed affordable housing units.

This entire legal process took more than twenty years and required great persistence and professionalism from the NRDC attorneys.

The NRDC attorneys believed that the Americans with Disabilities Act applied to the widespread presence of asthma and other respiratory illnesses caused by mold that affected so many tenants. The attorneys, working with NYCHA residents and Metro IAF leaders and staff, began to put together a major lawsuit based on the charge that neglect by NYCHA was triggering disabilities or worsening health outcomes for those with many already vulnerable or compromised health.

While continuing the classic Metro IAF on-the-ground organizing, a concerted effort by leaders and organizers began to document the conditions that would form the basis of the suit against the City of New York. Key leaders like Fr. Frank Skelly, Ray Lopez, Rev. Getulio Cruz, Maria Peguerro, Angel Diaz, and others joined tenant leaders like Bernard Smith, Luz Garcia, and Yaniris Diaz to gather the facts and find potential class representatives who both had asthma and were clearly affected by mold and nothing else. After eliminating smokers, individuals with other allergies, and even people with pets, for example, Metro IAF found three compelling representatives from a vast group of tenants who were suffering. They were NYCHA tenants Maribel Baez, Felipa Cruz, and Rosanna de La Cuadra, on behalf of her minor-age child.

Metro IAF built a class action lawsuit on behalf of all NYCHA tenants with asthma; and NRDC brought in the National Center for Law and Economic Justice (NCLEJ) because of their expertise in that particular area of the law.

KEEPING THE CONDITIONS IN NYCHA ON THE PUBLIC AGENDA

While preparations for the lawsuit continued, it was key to the success of this campaign that the issue stayed in the forefront of the minds of public officials who can make change and the media who influence them.

One reason that Metro IAF has always been reluctant to use the courts as a tactic is that a lawsuit usually takes many months (or even years) to prepare; and then the rhythm of the court system itself, often quite deliberate and subject to extended delays, takes over. So the challenge Metro IAF faced in this campaign was how to sustain and even expand the level of interest and attention to NYCHA's shortcomings while the legal team and plaintiffs were assembling the material that would be needed to mount an effective court challenge.

The answer was action. Metro IAF affiliates would invite NYCHA officials into well-organized, packed meetings of NYCHA residents where local leaders would press those officials to address specific key issues. In one dramatic example in 2012, South Bronx Churches held an assembly at Immaculate Conception Church and honored a NYCHA tenant, a non-smoker who had died of lung cancer while living in a mold-infested apartment that had never been properly remediated.

In December 2012, Metro IAF leaders held another large action at Monte Sion Christian Church in the East Village to publicly announce the "notice of intent to sue" NYCHA. Hundreds of people and scores of reporters heard tenants at that action tell their stories of struggling with asthma and NYCHA's inattention to their plight. Organizational leaders and attorneys then laid out the legal plan.

Because of its long history of dysfunction and the 'narrative' that NYCHA could never be improved, it was very difficult to sustain local press coverage on public housing unless a particularly outrageous event occurred (such as when a tiger was discovered living as a pet in an apartment) or unless the issue of NYCHA's future could be integrated into a more immediate public dynamic. That dynamic occurred in the mayoral race of 2013. First, Metro IAF leaders met with the editors of the *New York Daily News* and designed with them a series of large public mayoral forums in which NYCHA was a main theme.

One reporter in particular, Greg Smith then of the *Daily News*, proved to be relentless in his pursuit of NYCHA news. When our team first met him, Smith was working on stories about how a police officer had been shot in a NYCHA development in a location where a camera had been funded by the City Council but never installed. Metro IAF shared with Smith reams of documents and stories, not only of problems but also missed opportunities. Starting in 2012, the reporter also uncovered critical stories through other sources that dramatized the slow-motion tragedy being caused by deteriorating conditions in the Housing Authority, its lack of funding, and the lack of ability by its leadership to generate any positive motion. This reporting was critical in forcing real change. Smith has continued this dogged journalism at TheCity.nyc.

At the first public forum, in January of 2013, over 1,500 tenants, homeowners, clergy, and other leaders from around the five boroughs of New York City gathered to press all top candidates to announce their positions on preserving and developing public housing in the city. All major media were there, and leaders elevated critical issues, especially mold and leaks in NYCHA buildings. This, along with the Daily News' continuous coverage, helped make NYCHA a key part of the 2013 race.

As a result of this attention and the filing of the legal Notice of Intent, the Bloomberg administration, winding down its time at City Hall, started to make much stronger pledges to improve NYCHA. Unfortunately, these promises were largely ineffective. Metro IAF continued to increase the pressure by focusing on the immediate harm being done to tenants' health. This was particularly important given that Michael Bloomberg publicly identified himself as the "Public Health Mayor" and wanted that image to remain untarnished. For this and other reasons, his aides began to negotiate the terms of a legal settlement on the lawsuit with Metro IAF leaders and lawyers in earnest.

In December of 2013, just weeks before Mayor Bloomberg left office, Metro IAF and the City of New York reached a settlement. It required NYCHA to remediate mold and excess moisture properly within seven days for a simple repair and fifteen days for a complicated one in a targeted 95% of cases. Metro IAF knew that this would be a difficult standard to enforce, but at long last, it was the start of real accountability. It was also the only settlement that the Bloomberg Administration reached with any community organization—a sign of the seriousness with which the case was taken as well as the impact of the fine reporting done by the *New York Daily News* and other news outlets. On a snowy December 17, 2013, over 50 tenants, clergy, and other allies gathered outside the NYC courthouse for a press conference celebrating the agreement and dramatizing the need for real action.

The celebration was well earned. But the results proved to be disappointing. The settlement meant that Metro IAF had to work very closely with many of the same officials and managers who had resisted accountability for decades. The supposed public servants were often unhappy to be forced to comply with the terms of the settlement, and they expressed that unhappiness by dragging their feet. While we found the occasional manager or staff person who wanted to expedite improvements and address tenant needs, the culture of NYCHA, deeply entrenched over many mayoral administrations, was hostile or indifferent. In numerous meetings, NYCHA would show power point presentations about work they claimed to have completed, but Metro IAF's on-the-ground relationships in those buildings allowed leaders to fact check those claims immediately and in many cases they were found to be exaggerated or simply false.

Metro IAF leaders also took NYCHA officials on tours, so they could see for themselves what problems had been left uncorrected. This produced dramatic moments, especially with Carlos Laboy-Diaz, the NYCHA Executive VP for Operations. EBC and Metro IAF invited him to an assembly at Our Lady of Mercy Church. Tawana Myers, an EBC tenant leader, held up the umbrella her family had to use while in the bathroom because of constant leaks from the apartment above. The packed house was amused, appalled, and finally outraged by the lack of NYCHA response. Later, Metro IAF leaders Maria Peguerro, Oscar and Felipa Cruz, and Fr. Tom Fenlon took Laboy-Diaz on a tour in the South Bronx, where a very large rat scurried across their path!

The lawyers from NCLEJ also brought in Steve Edwards, a senior litigator, and many young attorneys, including Erin Meyer, all from the law firm Hogan Lovells, who did substantial and high-quality pro-bono work.

The creation of the settlement/consent decree and the increased press coverage led to an improvement in NYCHA response to specific problems brought to its attention. However, these periods of more reliable responsiveness were short-lived. NYCHA's culture reasserted itself. One tenant leader was told "we are only fixing your apartment because you are with South Bronx Churches. Don't tell anyone." Metro IAF of course told everyone who would listen, but we were too often stymied by the vastness of the NYCHA system and the limitations of an organizational presence in only about 20% of that world.

The new DeBlasio administration did nothing to correct the worst traits of NYCHA managers and officials. One NYCHA chairperson agreed to an experiment with Metro IAF. Leaders produced a list of 50 apartments with serious repair issues. In the weeks that followed, NYCHA went to work. When NYCHA announced that it was finished, Metro IAF leaders met with the chairwoman. She had been told that 47 of the 50 units had been successfully repaired. Metro IAF had documented each repair request and had taken photos of every issue. In fact, no more than five of the apartments had been properly repaired. The others were either poorly addressed or not addressed at all.

Our leaders told the chairwoman, "What you fail to understand is that staff lie or exaggerate. And the lies and exaggerations grow larger as they rise through the NYCHA system, so when they get to your office they are immense." She thanked the

Metro IAF team for pointing that out, promised to address it, and then did nothing, like so many people before her. Those within NYCHA who resented Metro IAF's work believed that they could simply wear the leaders down. This strategy had worked for decades. But Metro IAF leaders were not out of options.

FORCING NYCHA TO COMPLY WITH THE CONSENT DECREE

As it became clear that NYCHA was not making real progress, an expanded core team of lawyers and leaders went to work in 2015 preparing a motion before the federal judge in charge of the original case to demand NYCHA's compliance. The team added tenant leaders like Nellie Rivera and Dolores Hall. They worked closely with the sharp and responsive legal team, including many volunteers from Hogan Lovells as well as the NRDC veterans, who were joined by attorney Sara Imperiale. Together, they documented the worst examples of NYCHA's neglect by visiting apartments, talking with more tenants, taking photos, and preparing exhaustive briefs that showed NYCHA's overall failure to comply with the consent decree.

In this process, NYCHA demonstrated the lack of attention they gave this case and the problems behind it in several ways, including by sending a single attorney to court, and no one else. This contrasted with our competent team of litigators and the courtroom packed with tenant leaders. Our motion asked for NYCHA to be ordered to comply and to file its reports on-time, as well as for the appointment of a special master.

In December 2015, Judge William H. Pauley III ordered NYCHA to obey the decree and found that the authority was "in violation of the consent decree from the day it was entered." He also said a special master was needed to make compliance happen. In late January 2016, he chose Prof. Francis McGovern from Duke University. This ruling was further vindication of the quality of the complaints documented by the Metro IAF tenant and legal team. It was another indictment of NYCHA and its culture of resistance and delay.

All organizing is a process of dis-organizing and re-organizing. This is a familiar theme in all effective organizing, and truer in this effort than in most others. The Metro IAF tenant and legal team welcomed the special master, created a method of addressing mold complaints and compiling the data that indicated progress made, and fought for two revisions of the consent decree in the years that have followed his appointment. Professor McGovern began meeting with Metro IAF veteran leaders and emerging new leaders of the effort—including tenants like Pura Cruz and Jacqueline Holmes—to see firsthand the conditions in the buildings and to hear from those who lived there. He took the time to tour apartments throughout the city. And he met with NYCHA staff up and down the line. He also attended a public action with 250 leaders in the South Bronx on June 26, 2016, and committed to work with Metro IAF until the mold and leaks that plagued the system were addressed.

Throughout the earlier years, Metro IAF had benefited from the work of Bill Sothern and his company, Microecologies, experts at identifying the leaks that were the source of mold and correcting those conditions. Microecologies started to develop a standard procedure for mold. This included a process of effective leak detection and remediation techniques using proper equipment (which NYCHA had long resisted), as well as focusing on improving ventilation in bathrooms to reduce moisture build up.

In this work, Metro IAF met NYCHA employees like the former Deputy Bronx Director Tommy John, who in October of 2016 personally supervised the cleaning of the vents in the apartment of Oscar and Felipa Cruz (which were blocked by a huge amount of refuse, including old tin cans). The team also met with Conrad Vasquez, the then Manhattan Borough Director, who launched effective blitzes in Manhattan developments. Due to excellent leadership from tenants like Juan Pichardo, Jose Ramirez, Maria Roman, Lydia Sotomayor, and Matilde Nunez, well over 500 more work orders were closed in late 2016. More than 200 leaders gathered at Monte Sion Christian Church just after the 2016 presidential election, to celebrate this progress and dedicate themselves to non-partisan organizing.

However, even this cooperation was extremely difficult. Mr. John should not have had to personally supervise the repair of a vent. Moreover, while the Manhattan Borough staff did try, they didn't understand basics like, for example, why it was a problem that half the people in a community meeting couldn't understand what was discussed because of poor acoustics. They also needed the Metro IAF leaders and organizers to push them to actually approach the scores of tenants affected, many of whom were skeptical, that we brought to an outreach event. Further, once the flurry of repairs was over, local staff returned to the pattern of missed appointments and poor work. There were also other employees who actively tried to stand in the way of necessary reforms and blamed tenants at every turn.

In order to try to bring additional pressure for change, in mid-2015 Metro IAF approached then U.S. Attorney for the Southern District of New York, Preet Bharara, on a number of topics, including the need for NYCHA to be pushed to improve mold, leaks, and many other conditions. In 2016 and 2017, our team of clergy, community health workers and tenants took two separate US Attorneys (Bharara and Geoffrey Berman) and their staff on tours of NYCHA developments to point out problems connected to mold and leaks, lack of heat and hot water, pest infestation, and many other issues.

SENIOR APARTMENTS ON VACANT OR UNDERUSED NYCHA SITES

Metro IAF also periodically found ways to connect the NYCHA work with one of its other major priorities—the creation of new, affordable homes—to bring even more pressure to bear on the city. One critical angle involved NYCHA sites and the potential for 15,000 units of new senior housing.

Led by its longtime affiliate East Brooklyn Congregations, Metro IAF began an effort to force Mayor Bill de Blasio to take radical and substantial action to both repair NYCHA buildings and build affordable senior housing on unused NYCHA land. This would help to provide seniors with beautiful new apartments, and make their old apartments (which often had more bedrooms than the seniors needed due to children moving out) available for families languishing in shelters or in overcrowded and substandard tenements. Metro IAF identified scores of NYCHA sites that could support thousands of units of new senior housing.

Metro IAF gathered over 6,000 people at City Hall on October 9, 2017, and thousands more at a series of actions and city council budget hearings to secure money for senior housing. This led to Mayor DeBlasio committing to put hundreds of millions in the budget, but then breaking his promise.

After another series of actions in 2018 and 2019, De Blasio grudgingly agreed to actually allocate $125 million in additional funding. This led to the construction of hundreds of new units of affordable senior housing on NYCHA land. In May of 2024, one of the newest completed projects was unveiled at Sumner Houses in Brooklyn. Six other sites are currently in the pipeline. While this is not at the scale or pace that is possible or needed, it is a direct result of the work of the Metro IAF team. It also helped to gain further public support, especially from elected officials and the press, for the need for more repairs in the existing NYCHA developments.

REVISED CONSENT DECREE

During this same period, while very few tenants had yet seen benefit from the consent decree, NYCHA told us none of the reforms they were designing with Microecologies would come into place until after April of 2018, when the consent decree would expire. In the meantime, one of our key attorneys, Erin Meyer, then having moved to Proskauer Rose, engaged Neil Steinkamp of Stout Risius Ross, to analyze NYCHA's quarterly reports. He discovered that NYCHA was misunderstanding their own data and radically overstating their already-low success rate in dealing with mold and leaks. It became clear that tenants needed immediate change. A new consent decree was necessary. Steve Edwards proposed the creation of an ombudsperson to whom tenants could appeal if their mold and leaks were not fixed in 15 days. This person would have the power to ensure required repairs were made.

In May of 2018, Metro IAF and NYCHA reached an agreement for a revised consent decree that drastically strengthened NYCHA's obligation to meet mold and leak remediation targets. It created strong independent oversight that included the ombudsperson: an independent data analyst who could see the entire flow of work, response, repairs, or lack of response, and what needed to change, as well as an independent mold analyst who could direct NYCHA on how best to eliminate mold.

Judge Pauley approved the settlement (after some modification) in November of 2018, with all the oversight measures that Metro IAF sought. In essence, Metro IAF leaders and lawyers designed and imposed a new system of accountable response and remediation that NYCHA would never have adopted on its own or implemented effectively.

This was one of several points where we had to ensure some of our very talented litigators that they understood that, as important as legal moves are, the courtroom was only one front in this campaign. In this case the judge, elected officials and the general public needed to understand how much our consent decree was rooted in tenant concerns and tenant leadership. While this is never a fully resolved tension, the lawyers definitely understood this and helped us to organize three separate events where we helped scores more tenants write letters to the court about their support for the settlement. This provided opportunities to engage new tenants and helped the people who testified and organized these events to develop their leadership skills.

YET ANOTHER LAYER OF ACTIVITY... WITH NEW PLAYERS

Metro IAF worked to get the right people in place to implement the new consent decree. In 2019, NYCHA agreed fairly quickly to appoint the firm of Stout Risius Ross (led by Neil Steinkamp and Kiersten Acevedo) as the Independent Data Analyst and Microecologies (led by Bill Sothern and Chris Mikrut) as the Independent Mold Analyst. They continued their work to build a real infrastructure for improvement.

Their work became somewhat easier because, in order to comply with the decree and other obligations, NYCHA brought in new staffers to do key work on this case and related issues. This included Vlada Kenniff, an experienced civil servant and urban planner, and Daniel Greene, a long time environmental lawyer. We didn't always agree with these new NYCHA officials, but it was clear they were working hard to make improvements.

The critical work of determining how the new court-appointed Ombudsperson would work was the most challenging thing to figure out. We jointly interviewed several candidates with NYCHA and finally agreed on a former assistant district attorney and criminal defense attorney named Cesar De Castro. The idea was that De Castro would work with the Stout Risius Ross firm, who would start an Ombudsperson Call Center (OCC). Any tenant who had reported mold or leaks that hadn't been dealt with properly in fifteen days could call in. The OCC would start by helping to facilitate communication in order to avoid the most common (fixable) problem of missed appointments by NYCHA employees, as well as tracking to ensure work was getting done. If that didn't suffice, the case would be escalated to the Ombudsperson. If necessary, he would issue an order or hire outside contractors (at NYCHA's expense) to ensure repairs were made.

Metro IAF continued meeting with tenants, documenting issues, and briefing people on this opportunity. On September 13th, there was a hearing regarding the status of the case and the appointment of De Castro as Ombudsperson, along with the approval of the Ombudsperson Call Center (OCC). When asked by press before the hearing, Metro IAF told the truth that very few tenants had seen improvement as a result of the consent decree but that the hope was that the Ombudsperson would change this. NYCHA attorneys were quite upset. However, this honesty was critical for gaining credibility with other tenant leaders and elected officials who would be key in implementing the oversight successfully. A week later the judge approved the appointment of De Castro.

De Castro, Stout Risius Ross, and NYCHA then started to prepare. The OCC was opened at the Jefferson Houses in November 2019. Staff from Little Sisters of the Assumption Family Health Services (a key Metro IAF member organization), Ray Lopez, Mario Bravo, Sergio Galvez, and others played a critical role in helping the OCC develop protocols and ensure they could communicate effectively with tenants. By January 2020, it was clear the program was working, and it started to expand. It was available citywide that July.

This took substantial effort from Metro IAF, as NYCHA at first wanted to roll it out a development at a time, which would have taken decades. But it helped that then Council Member Ritchie Torres wrote a bill requiring that everyone who lived in NYCHA be notified about the OCC. A group of Metro IAF tenants and other leaders stood with him outside the Millbrook Houses (where the OCC was already available) to announce the bill. This effective action generated press coverage and public interest that ensured NYCHA had to expand the OCC roll out more rapidly.

Metro IAF also successfully pushed for concrete changes, like a real commitment to fix ventilation which Bill Sothern identified as the cause of roughly 30% of NYCHA's mold. NYCH allowed Vlada Kenniff to work with Microecologies. They made slow steady progress, which eventually helped lead to major reduction in new mold complaints.

RESULTS TO DATE

The relentless pressure exerted by determined NYCHA tenants and other Metro IAF local leaders has been the thread that has kept this complicated and extended campaign on target over several decades. The engagement of top professionals like Neil Steinkamp and Bill Sothern—independent experts committed to concrete evaluation and improvement—gave the Metro IAF team the kind of information and evaluation that strengthened its case at every step of the way. The work of indefatigable attorneys like Steve Edwards, Erin Meyer, Nancy Marks, Al Huang, and Sara Imperiale, as well as many new attorneys, made it possible to work effectively with the two federal judges and two special masters and others in the legal system. This persistence had to endure through the passing of key people, like tenant leader Felipa Cruz; Steve Edwards and Tommy John of NYCHA; as well as the first

Judge and Special Master, Judge Pauley and Prof. McGovern.

However, the broad team of dedicated people meant progress could continue. The creation of the Ombudsperson Call Center (OCC) and other methods of tracking NYCHA responses and repairs means that tenants are finally able to get better and more reliable reactions to their complaints. Finally, the cooperation of several key NYCHA staff members, often involving tension with other NYCHA officials, made progress possible that had been delayed too long.

So here are the results to date in real numbers:

- 30,000 families have benefited from repairs that upgraded ventilation and properly fixed mold and leaks; as a result, there has been a 50% decrease in mold and leak complaints.
- 125,000 work tickets for mold and leak problems have been legitimately closed, another indicator of the effectiveness of the systems created by Metro IAF tenant and community leaders.

- 22,000 residents participated in forty-three public actions, countless tenant and community meetings, and countless smaller sessions with elected officials, health professionals, legal experts, and others
- 150 media and opinion pieces have made sure that the NYCHA challenge and the Metro IAF response to that challenge emerged as an important theme in New York City's dynamic and hectic media environment.

CONCLUSION

Four Strategies That Produced Real Change

What Metro IAF in New York City did over many years, relying overwhelmingly on volunteer leaders supported by a small staff of organizers who often had additional priorities, was the following:

- Built, trained, and expanded a base of tenant leaders and supporters who brought their direct experiences of NYCHA failures to the task of creating real change.
- Worked with a team of attorneys to threaten a class-action lawsuit and negotiate a settlement in federal court. Worked with the judge and a special master to make sure that the terms of the settlement were

met. When they weren't met, Metro IAF leaders and attorneys designed revised consent decrees that were reviewed and adopted by the judge.
- Developed a team of allies—City Councilman and now Congressman Ritchie Torres, Congressman Hakeem Jeffries, Senator Charles Schumer, and others—who pressured NYCHA alongside Metro IAF.
- Recruited and helped deploy a team of experts in mold, leaks, and data collection and evaluation to create an effective external system of oversight and accountability that guaranteed NYCHA's compliance.

Juggling and managing these four aspects of a sustained campaign, year after year, was demanding, as you might expect. But without all four of these approaches, any hope of reforming NYCHA and creating conditions that benefited the tenants would have failed.

To say more work needs to be done is to say the least. Superficial responses—from privatization that has proven to be mixed at best or the wishful hope for scores of billions of public funds that are not likely ever to appear—still circulate among those who have no understanding of the critical importance of revitalizing NYCHA and making it a healthy and safe housing option for more than half a million New Yorkers.

But more than 30,000 families are better off today than they were because of the work of Metro IAF. Our team, having proven that progress can and will be made, continues to tackle all false promises and press for meaningful and verifiable improvements in the nation's largest and most important concentration of truly public housing.

BOOKS ON LEADERSHIP

Bending Granite
30+ true stories of leading change
compiled by Tom Mosgaller, et. al.

Ed Marciniak's City and Church
A Voice of Conscience
by Charles Shanabruch

The Heartbeat of Wounded Knee
Native America from 1890 to Present
by David Treuer

Lessons Learned
Stories from a Lifetime in Organizing
by Arnie Graf

Our Birthright
The Politics of Jesus for Black People Today
by Keisha Krumm

Reveille for a New Generation
Organizers and Leaders Reflect on Power
compiled by Gregory Pierce

Sometimes David Wins
Organizing to Overcome "Fated Outcomes"
by Frank C. Pierson, Jr.

Song in a Weary Throat
Memoir of an American Pilgrimage
by Pauli Murray

www.actapublications.com, 800-397-2282

BOOKLETS ON ORGANIZING

Going to the Well to Build Community
by Deacon Timothy E. Tilghman

How to Raise Money for Your Organization and
Raising Money for Your Congregation
by Robert Connolly

***Lessons from One Campaign
for Game-Changing School Reform***
by Raymond Domanico

People's Institutions in Decline and
Freedom from and Freedom For and
Effective Organizing for Congregational Renewal
by Michael Gecan

The Power of Relational Action and
Action Creates Public Life
by Ed Chambers

Mixing It Up in the Public Arena
by A. Zeik Saidman

Rebuilding Our Institutions
by Ernesto Cortes, Jr.

Reflecting with Scripture on Community Organizing
by Rev. Jeffrey K. Krehbiel

***Using the Tools of Community Organizing to Build
Your Union's Strength in the Post-Janus Era***
Jonathan Lange, Amy Vruno, Ben Gordon

www.actapublications.com, 800-397-2282